Monk Mode

Be More By Doing Less

Mésac Adna

© **Copyright 2016 by VisProject - All rights reserved.**

This document is geared towards providing exact and reliable information in regards to the topic and issue covered. The publication is sold with the idea that the publisher is not required to render accounting, officially permitted, or otherwise, qualified services. If advice is necessary, legal or professional, a practiced individual in the profession should be ordered.

- From a Declaration of Principles which was accepted and approved equally by a Committee of the American Bar Association and a Committee of Publishers and Associations.

In no way is it legal to reproduce, duplicate, or transmit any part of this document in either electronic means or in printed format. Recording of this publication is strictly prohibited and any storage of this document is not allowed unless with written permission from the publisher. All rights reserved.

The information provided herein is stated to be truthful and consistent, in that any liability, in terms of inattention or otherwise, by any usage or abuse of any policies, processes, or directions contained within is the solitary and utter responsibility of the recipient reader. Under no circumstances will any legal responsibility or blame be held against the publisher for any reparation, damages, or monetary loss due to the information herein, either directly or indirectly.

Respective authors own all copyrights not held by the publisher.

The information herein is offered for informational purposes solely, and is universal as so. The presentation of the information is without contract or any type of guarantee assurance.

The trademarks that are used are without any consent, and the publication of the trademark is without permission or backing by the trademark owner. All trademarks and brands within this book are for clarifying purposes only and are the owned by the owners themselves, not affiliated with this document.

Introduction

Today's generation has been the most fortunate of any generation prior. Most of the daily struggles that plagued humanity has quickly disappeared in the modern world. The citizens of the civilized nations have the courtesy of the most economic flexibility available in human history. By working hard (and a bit of luck), it is possible to alter the course of one's life. Despites the ever increasing economic and social disparities (which does irrefutably exist), there is still more economic fluidity than in any of the previous centuries. It is possible for a poor child living in rural Mississippi to become a multi-millionaire. It is possible for an immigrant refuge in the U.S to climb up the social ladder and become a doctor. The homeless person in the street can turn their lives around. It is not easy, and even in the United States, not everyone shares the same starting line. But despite how low the probability is, success is possible for every citizen of the modern world. The peasant living in the Dark Ages had zero chances of ever achieving royalty. They were stuck in their social status from birth all the way to their death. However, even with all of these new opportunities, most people still find themselves unhappy with their lives. <u>The happiness index is at an all-time low.</u> Why is that? While there are many nuances to the cause of the unhappiness of the populace, the main problem is this:

→ *People are not living the fulfilling life that they envisioned of themselves*←

"I want to leave my job"
"I want to find that significant other"
"I want to write a book"
"I want to start a business"
"I want to be spiritually fulfilled"
"I want to learn a new language"

These are goals that people have and try their hardest to achieve, and when they don't achieve them, regardless of the opportunities at hand, they will feel unsatisfied and unhappy.

There are reasons why people fail at achieving their goals, and we will address them in this book. But the real question is whether there is a proven way to create the life that you want and to achieve your goals. While there is no shortcut or 'for sure' methods, there are mindsets that can greatly increase your chances to achieve fulfillment. This book will describe one such method. In this book, we will introduce and explain the framework of Monk Mode.

Monk Mode can be seen as a juncture in which you dedicate your entire attention towards your goal. It is a time where you cultivate better habits and tools necessary for self-actualization. Monk Mode does come with temporary sacrifices, which will be discussed throughout the book, but the benefits are enormous.

Monk Mode is generally divided into three transitional periods, which are called the three I's.
Introspection, Isolation, and Improvement.
The first period is introspection, which is the developmental stage where one evaluates themselves and processes the changes that needs to be done in their life. Introspection may very well be the most crucial part of MM. The second period is isolation, this is the meat of Monk Mode, where one will alienate themselves from distractions. Distractions can be from outside influences and from the inside (daydream much?). The better the isolation is, the more efficient the Monk Mode will be. Isolation doesn't necessarily mean total reclusion from everyone and everything. It is isolation from 'draining' activities. The last period of Monk Mode is Improvement, which is the implementation of self-improving activities. Without having a great improvement plan, which is done during introspection, Monk Mode will not be effective. With these three I's, Monk Mode can help you achieve your goals.

I have undergone many Monk Modes, and it has proven to be an essential part to my own development and success. I hope to bring this tool to you in full form, so that it may do the same for you. Thank you for purchasing this book, and I hope that it brings value to your life.

Chapter 1

The Reasons of Failure

Before we can address a solution to why people fail at achieving their goals, we must identify the causes of failure. Throughout this book, I will be giving examples of people that I have encountered in my life. These people have had a big effect on my success. This is because some of them inspired me and showed me the correct habits and attitude to obtain; while others showed me the exact things not to encompass. It all began in college. I had a friend in undergrad who told me of his goal of becoming an engineer. He seemed like a bright guy, and had a concrete plan on how he was going to succeed. He was a nice guy, and we would sometimes study together. Ultimately though, he had to drop out of the program after his second year. As a freshman, I didn't want to suffer his fate, so I wrote down his tendencies in a black journal. The journal was initially to remind myself of what habits not to have, but it also later became a journal about habits that are necessary for long term success. Due to these constructive habits, I shared many successes in college. I kept the journal to myself, until my very last year.

My senior year, I met a woman who had ambitions and tremendous potential, but didn't have the necessary habits. She came to me asking for advice on how to ameliorate herself. At the time, I was very busy and couldn't tutor her individually. So, I decided to do something that I had never done before. I let her borrow my black journal. I didn't have any real expectations that the journal would help her, it was just my own scribblings and rants. But I thought that it would maybe give her a nudge in the right direction. Time flew by, and I forgot about this whole exchange. A couple of month later, that same woman came to me with my black journal in her hands, and said:

" *Mésac, this journal is amazing.*"

" *What do you mean?*", I asked.

"It has literally changed my lifestyle. The reasons that you wrote about why your friend failed, the philosophy that aided you to succeed, and this Monk Mode stuff... this is really good material. You should share this with others"

I was pleased that my journal helped her, and promised her that I would try to share it with as many people as I could. This book, is for the most part, a refined version of my black journal. In my journal, I detailed three reasons why most people fail at achieving their goals. The reasons are the three fears:

1. Fear of Failure
2. Fear of Truth
3. Fear of Loneliness

Fear of Failure

The first obstacle that interferes with people is their fear of failure. This is the fear that people have about contemplating becoming more than what they currently are and failing. It is a fear of realizing an inadequacy, and therefore being unable to fix it. Most people are content living in their bubbles, and not challenging their thoughts on reality. If they opened their eyes to the other side of the mirror, they may not like what they see. Change always comes with risks, the risk of failure. Failure can lead to disappointment and humiliation, which are things that people want to avoid. What is the best way to avoid failure?

"By not trying"

I have met many people who have told me that they didn't try x and y because they wanted to stay realistic. This is a symptom of *the fear of failure*. Realism is mostly a construct. How many successful people has ever said that they became what they are due to realism? You will be hard pressed to find one. Success does not come from normalcy, or adherence to it, but from deviation and experimentation. Experimentation comes with risks. When running a business, a person has to risk the money that is invested in that business. The risk of losing that money is scary, but should not be a deterrent from achieving one's most desired goal. It is better to try and fail, than to regret later.

Fear of Truth

The second reason that most people fail at their goals is that they fear the truth. The truth that they may not be adept at what they are trying to do. Or that they are going about it the wrong way. Being realistic is a deterrent for most people, but they are some situations that are just not practical.
Here are two examples:

a. The 5ft tall, 26 year old man, with a 12 inch vertical that has aspirations to make it to the NBA.
b. The college kid who wants to become a nuclear physicist, but is struggling with using the quadratic formula.

There is a great deal of worth about being persistent and resilient. "Fail 11 times, and get back up 12" is a valuable concept that is key to achieving success in any field. However, very rarely will you see anyone who is completely mediocre, with no potential, at something suddenly become a master at it. Unfortunately, the 26-year-old man will not be able to play in the NBA, the average height of professional basketball players is 6'7ft with an average vertical leap of 32-inches. This man does not even measure up with the physical averages of a middle school basketball team. Of course, it is *certainly possible* that through a miraculous event, he makes it in the NBA. But the probability would be well under 1 percent. It is that ludicrous. Telling the man to give up on that goal would be doing him justice, it is more likely that he has gift doing something else.

The college student who wants to become a nuclear physicist is also better off picking a new major. Physics is a difficult subject in which several other disciplines are involved. However, the core of physics is mathematics. It is not necessary to be a math genius to become an excellent nuclear physicist, but it is needed to be well above average. The nuclear physicists are the ones who not only excel at mathematics, but wanted to apply those mathematical concepts to an applicable field. This suggests that mathematics is only a foundational knowledge that allows a person to then apply it to real world problems. Lower level physics deals with computational mathematics, with some background theory involved. Higher level physics involves theoretical probability and mathematics, with abstract applications. The abstract applications of nuclear physics involve using particle colliders and advanced computer software. A college student who has difficulty comprehending the quadratic formula (which is a high school Algebra I concept) will have an even tougher time understanding derivatives and integrals, let alone the higher level mathematics and statistics that comes with physics. Again, it is possible that there is some chance that everything will eventually 'click', but the chances are very low. It is important to not waste time, and focus on hard but achievable goals.

The advice to not be realistic is sometimes mistaken with lacking to be practical. Everyone has their path and fate, and life is the easiest when one finds their niche and ameliorate from there. The inability to figure out and accept one's own limits and capacity is a reason why people fail at fulfillment. They aren't thinking hard enough about the pragmatism of their dreams, and therefore waste precious time. The sad part is that most are unwilling to face reality even when it hits them. This was the case with another buddy of mine in college:

As you can see, I have met many interesting people in my years in undergraduate. But none as interesting as this particular man. Lance. Lance is a man that I met through extracurricular activities. Virtually every night, I would go to the gym to play pick-up basketball. There were always many regulars, and I was one as well. We all got to know each other pretty well, and Lance took a liking to me. We started hanging-out outside of the gym, and I got to know his personal life. Lance was a great speaker, and very funny too. Though he had a couple of weird habits, he seemed like a reasonable guy. His major was pre-law, and he wanted to go

Harvard Law after his studies at his current college. That is definitely a high aspiration, and a goal worthy to be respected. Harvard law is surely one, if not, the toughest law school to get into. I expected Lance to be an extremely focused and balanced young man. I was surprised to see that this wasn't the case. Lance was single, and it wasn't by choice. He desperately wanted to have a girlfriend, but the project eluded him. He would start going to the bar as early as Thursday night, and party all throughout the weekend. He would download all sort of dating apps, and would sometimes roams the hallways at night looking for a girl to strike a conversation with (I know...). All to increase his chances of meeting a girl that would take him. I found this to be very peculiar, but I didn't say anything about it. The more I got to know Lance, I started to see other things as well. He was the ultimate procrastinator, and would very often not only start writing his homework and term papers the day it was due, but sometimes the day AFTER it was due. His professors were very lenient with him. His basketball hobby also wasn't just directed to pick up basketball, he would play NBA2k for hours on end during the day, and skip classes to play in video-game tournaments.

As I observed all of this, I remembered him telling me about his aspirations to go to Harvard Law.

Giving him the benefit of the doubt, I assumed that he had a plan on how to achieve this. I asked him his GPA.

He told me it was a 2.3, on a scale of 4.0. I was shocked. Surely if he was a genius, it would make more sense to me for him to have such bad habits. His outstanding GPA would balance everything out. Bafflingly, this man was borderline failing his program, and still held aspirations for Harvard Law! Was he serious?

I told myself that maybe he didn't understand how competitive such a program would be. Maybe he needed a wakeup call. I decided to do that for him. I had a very serious conversation with him about his habits, and how unless he dramatically changed, he wouldn't get into Harvard Law. He looked at me, shrugged, and defiantly said, "I'll make it Harvard Law, don't tell me what I can and cannot do"
I left him alone after that.
Needless to say, Lance didn't make it into Harvard Law nor any law schools.

This is an extreme case, but to some degree, people do fear the truth. The truth can be good sometimes, but other times it may not be. The truth can sometime be that your window of opportunity has passed. Or that you don't have the natural talent for a particular field. If that is the case, IT IS OK. You can find another field that suits your talents better. Deliberately deluding one selves is a recipe for disaster. Do not be like Lance. Please do not be like Lance.

The Fear of Loneliness

The third and last fear that I noticed and wrote down in my journal is *the fear of loneliness*. This is the fear of leaving people behind or being accused of "selling out". This fear has stopped people in cold tracks from achieving their goals. They are afraid of what others will think of them. They are afraid of losing people.

"Birds of a Feather Flock Together"

People that share the same economic, social, physical, and spiritual status tend to congregate together. The rich have meetings and dinner with other rich people. The poor tend to stay with other poor. Religious groups stay together, since they share the same epistemology. This is a common attribute of humankind. It is comfortable to stay with similar people, that is, until you try to stray from the pack…

Lucy's goal is to lose 45 pounds in the next 6 months. She has decided to go into Monk Mode to achieve this goal. Most of her friends are overweight, and have unhealthy eating habits. They too have had plans of losing weight for years, but never attained much success. Lucy loves her friends and they do a lot together. They even have nights where they binge on ice cream and Netflix. They also all work out every Wednesday morning together. They have fun doing all of these activities, but Lucy is worried. Her weight hasn't decreased at all in the past year. It has increased, and her family has a history of diabetes. She doesn't want to fall into her hereditary trap. She needs to lose weight, no matter what. She wants to obtain healthy habits that can sustain healthy living for years. Lucy understands that becoming serious about losing weight will have to be a solitary project. She is aware of the effort, work, and discipline necessary to get control of her life. She knows what it takes, but she also knows that her friends aren't ready for that sort of commitment. She cannot wait for them to be ready, she must get control of her weight now! She feels bad about leaving them behind, and wonders about what they will they think of her? Will they be happy? Jealous? Will they have anything in common again, she won't be able to enjoy the ice cream and netflix binge. This realization makes Lucy cringe. She doesn't want to alienate her friends. She decides to tell them about her Monk Mode plan and asked them to participate too, but it would have to be a solitary thing. The group of friends agree. Lucy is pleased, she won't have to leave her friends behind, in six months, they will all have lost weight and obtained valuable habits. Unfortunately, this didn't happen. Lucy did manage to lose a significant amount of weight in six months, she lost around 38 pounds. She also gained very healthy eating habits that will sustain her. These habits have been so ingrained in her that there aren't even a chore anymore, she does them out of will. Her friends didn't share the same fate. They didn't lose any weight. They gave up on Monk Mode months ago. They even had their ice cream and Netflix binge night without Lucy.

Lucy was devastated when she found out, but she figured that this would happen. She knew that her friends weren't ready. But Lucy wasn't ready either. During the six months of Monk Mode, Lucy's friend had become weary of her. They were sick of hearing about the No Carbs diet that she was on, or how her boyfriend helped her work out regularly. Lucy realized that she wasn't losing touch with her friends, now that she had taken a positive step in her *life, she no longer had the same things in common with them.*

We are social creatures; we enjoy each other's company more than we think. We want to belong to a group, and like minds congregate. If this feeling of unity isn't unconditional, or near-unconditional, then it can fall apart. All it took for Lucy to lose her unity with her friends was to fundamentally change her habits towards health, diet, and fitness. While doing that, she raised her awareness and lost the connecting tie of ignorance once shared with her friends. Lucy, then, may feel lonely.

The *fear of loneliness* is real, but unfounded. I cannot promise that your friends will acclimate to your changes, but I can say that you will able to find like-minded people. You will not be alone. Your priority shouldn't be on what others think of you, but instead of self-improvement. What can you do for yourself? Once you have improved yourself, your true friends will stick around and you will make new friends. Friends shouldn't be there simply to share misery, but should also be there to congratulate and be inspired by you and vice versa.

Distractions

A consequence of having a *fear of loneliness* is being tempted to overcompensate by becoming susceptible to distractions. Distractions are one of the most potent forces keeping most from actualizing their goals. It is such a damper on productivity that Monk Mode in its basic form is a method created to cut out all unnecessary distractions. Some distractions are good, and can even be constructive, but most are a poison to productivity. Previous studies have shown that distractions not only add time to projects that you want completed, but also dulls the quality of the work that ultimately produced.

What are some distractions?
1. People
2. Content (Music, T.V Shows, Movies)
3. Social Media (Facebook, Twitter, etc..)
4. Daydreaming
5. Food

There are many more.
These distractions, for some, are ways to cope with their fear of loneliness. How can you feel lonely when having access to millions of people in social media? Or having endless streaming shows that can entertain you for days on end? Everyone has that one friend that talks a little bit too much, and can eat away time like a plate of ribs. When you add up all the distractions that stray into our daily life, it is incredible that we get anything

done at all. It is overwhelming. Shutting off the television, or deactivating your social media, is scary to some. It has become a dependency; people do not want to lose their access to the distractions. Doing so will force them to become introspective. Introspection can lead to pain. That is a very psychological way to say that obsession with distractions is a form of fear, but it is necessary to break it down in this manner. The perfect example to demonstrate this is Lance. Lance, not only, had a fear of the truth, but was afraid of being lonely. He was always looking for distractions. If he wasn't eating lunch with a fraternity (whom he didn't belong to), he was playing video games with people in the game room. If he wasn't roaming dorms looking for open doors (to talk to people), he was playing pick-up basketball. He was at the bar almost every night, and would sleep in other's dorm room, and rarely his own. There was even a time, where I was done studying for an exam, and it was very late at night-roughly around 3am. As I was walking back to my dorm from a study room, I saw him roaming the building alone with clearly no direction. Just looking for someone or something to distract him.

Lance was a friend, and I cared for him...but he undeniably had a fear of being alone, and he would search out every possible distraction to keep him from that reality.

Lance had issues deeper than I'm discussing, but I'm using an extreme case again to make a general point: We are addicted to distractions. This addiction is similar to refine sugar addiction.

Refined sugar has no nutritional value, and it does not add anything substantive to our lives. It is actually taking away and eroding our overall health. But the populace is addicted to the substance. It is literally everywhere. Even hot dogs and hamburgers contain refined sugar. It is an ingredient that, as a society, let become a part of our daily diet when it shouldn't be. Distractions are equivalent. It provides very little value to our overall goal, but like sugar, it feels good. It feels good to binge on Netflix, or gossip with your friends for hour on end. Those may feel good temporarily, but over the long term, it will leave you with regret. Distractions are probably closing your doors on opportunities. They must be cut out.

Like previously said, Monk Mode in its purest form is a way to expel all unnecessary distractions. Think of yourself being a smartphone. Just imagine it for a second. You are a smartphone, and you have all of these apps (or activities) running at one time competing for your attention (battery life). Your battery life is being drained and depleted due to all of these running apps. Monk Mode is battery saver mode. It is the mode where all of the apps draining your battery life is extinguished and only the core and necessary applications are running. To go back on humanistic terms, all distractions that are plaguing your life's energy: people, social media, obsessions, are all turned off (some permanently, some only temporarily) and you get a chance to focus on yourself. Now with all of the background information in check, let's get to the methodology of Monk Mode.

Chapter 2
Introspection

When first entering Monk Mode, the most critical step in determining your success will be the first period: introspection. Introspection is the therapeutic and planning part of your sabbatical. It is the moment where you sit down, and just think about what you need to change. You ask yourself, "what is the problem that I want to fix?". Failing to clearly identify the problem at hand will make it impossible to formulate an appropriate plan of attack.

A good exercise to really hammer out what you believe you need to change is to take a notepad and sit down. Take away all distractions. Then, write about your insecurities and your worries. Have two distinct categories.
- a. *Worries that you cannot inherently change*
- b. *Worries that you can change through effort*

Worries that you cannot inherently change

No matter how much you try, there are some aspects of yourself that you cannot inherently change. An example of this would be certain physical traits. If you feel that you were born too short and thus are unattractive, then too bad, there isn't much that you can do about that. Height is predetermined by your genetics. Your doctor can tell from birth how tall you are going to be approximately. So changing the physical trait of height is not possible. However, it may be possible to mitigate the conclusion of that unchangeable feature. Meaning that though you cannot get taller, the problem isn't inherently that you want to be tall. It is that you feel like you aren't attractive due to the lack of height. The only option to mitigate that conclusion is to compensate. Unfortunately, you aren't getting any taller, so you can try to dress better. This will boost your attraction level. Or you can start an intense weightlifting workout routine, after gaining some muscle, it may compensate for the lack in the vertical axis.

If a person wishes that that they were German, but they weren't born or have any ancestry linking them to Germany, then it will be impossible for them to be German. It is not a reality that can be achieved, it is inherently true that they aren't German. That's never going to change. However, if they truly want to connect with the German culture, they can learn the language, study the customs, make German friends, and plan a trip there. They can immerse themselves into German-hood, and compensate. They can marry a German person, and have half-German kids. These things will never make them German, but they will be able to get as close to it as possible.

Worries that you can change through effort

There are other aspects of yourself that can be changed through sheer effort. If you want to write a screenplay, that IS something that can be achieved. If a person has an unhealthy addiction, that is also something that can be fundamentally changed. Other things that can be changed are

Learning a new language *Wanting more friends*
Losing Weight *Being More Funny*
Saving Money *Wanting to have more Friends*
Acing an exam

These are all examples of goals that people make all of the time. They worry about these things, but they sometimes forget that they have control over them. They are not like the worries discussed in the previous paragraph. These are things that can be changed. You will need to make a plan and a timeline of how you will achieve this. The emphasis is to be realistic, while still pushing yourself. Monk Mode will be a time where what would normally take longer decreases.

Here's an example of this process:

Goal: To Lose 20 pounds in 3 month

How→ time: 3 month → Diet: No Carbs→ Working out:3x a week, cardio & weight lifting

After this rough sketch, you can add to your list the exact dates that you will work out and times. Also write down an approximate amount of money that will be spend. Figure out which gym you will attend, how you will get there. Buy a book on dieting on *No Carbs*, or even hire a nutritionist to help you along the way.

When you have been able to do a rough sketch of the details and preparations. You are ready to move on to the next step.

Chapter 3 Isolation
Estranging The World

Isolation is a very important part of Monk Mode. It is what people think of first when Monk Mode is mentioned. They may have a vision of some disheveled man going out to the wilderness to find himself. Isolation doesn't have to mean that. Isolation is the time where you start estranging yourself from the world. You look at the world, and decide to take a timeout. You limit your interactions with reality significantly. In reference to the smartphone analogy, you go into power saving mode.

Current events, politics, social life are all important but they will have to take a backseat and be dramatically reduced. Reality has a million things trying to catch our attention, some of them are important but most aren't pertinent. Damage to the ecosystem is very important, and we should care about the state of the planet for our grandchildren but this issue is not pertinent to us directly. It is not an immediate concern.

Taking a break from current events doesn't mean total denial that things are going on outside of your personal bubble. That would be dangerous and counterproductive. The key is to limit your interactions with the news world that will shove the same story line in your face for 9 hours straight, with the only change being a new host every hour. Or you will be glued to Facebook or Twitter that will distract you with deliberate polarization and misinformation. While in Monk Mode [and this, honestly, would be a good practice to have permanently] you will want to just digest the main story line without all of the fluff around it.

The news are filled with horrible stories of despair, delinquencies, depravity, and hopelessness. Watching a constant stream of that will put you in that same mindset. If you feel hopelessness and despair after a day of watching cable news how do you suppose you will find the determination to achieve your goal?...I'll give you a hint...you won't.

Here are some good tips in taking your digital sabbatical.
- a. Detox once in a while
    - i. Have set amount of time where you do not consume bad news, try to balance yourself out by immersing yourself on positive storylines. People can be bad and do evil, but people can also do beautiful and good things. This shouldn't be lost.
- b. Don't watch cable T.V
    - i. For most, this will be self-explanatory, but please don't worry yourself with cable news. They are all funded by private interests, and are completely biased in

their reporting and talking points. Watching cable news will literally rot your brain.
   c. Delete social media
      i. More on this soon, but like cable t.v, social media is riddle with ignorance and misinformation. It is best to completely avoid that.
   d. Just Get the Headlines
      i. It is all that you need to be informed. Read the headline for the stories of that day and keep it moving.

Even without monk mode, this practice would improve your mood and make you more productive. It is necessary to keep your mood controlled in Monk Mode, but it's a good habit to be maintain throughout your life.

Outside Obligations

The key thing about Monk Mode is that you are living without excess for a short period of time. This mean that you want to cut out anything deemed unnecessary. The eastern monks go out in reclusion for a preset amount of time to totally tune out the distractions. I know someone who decided to live with the Amish for a year for his Monk Mode. Ideally, we would all choose to find a getaway spot in Hawaii and do our Monk Mode there. But the reality is that we are all not able to have a break from work for a year, some cannot afford to take a week break from their jobs. For some, the reason why they need Monk Mode is to find a way out of their economic hardship. Monk Mode provides an opportunity to achieve financial freedom and to live a better life.

Therefore, the degree in which one limits their outside obligation will differ from person to person. One may be able to completely make a getaway to a vacation spot and isolate themselves totally. Another person may only be able to take a 3-4 weeks paid vacation, others, though may not be able to postpone their jobs at all. That is not a problem. Monk Mode can be done regardless of which isolation intensity you choose. The distinction has to be made, though, between necessary and unnecessary activities. Is your job necessary? Probably. Is going to Bingo night every Tuesday and Thursday night necessary? Probably not. Isolation means different things for different folks. An extrovert may be better off letting some outside light come into the room. An introvert may be more comfortable totally alienating themselves for a while.

You want time to be on your side when you are in Monk Mode. Having too many outside obligations will get in the way of that. My friend Derrick is the perfect example of that.

Derrick is a very inspirational man, a big influence in my own life. He kept himself very busy, as he was the president or vice president of over six clubs, and owned several successful businesses. He also consistently worked out, and made sure to make time for an active social life. However, he had a goal to self-teach himself software coding. He had found the perfect program that would allow him to know the basics of a popular software language in less than four weeks. He was adamant about adding the course into his schedule, and he did. But he wasn't able to go through the program successfully. All of his other obligations got in the way. He would constantly be called into meetings. He would have exams and projects that would takes weeks to prepare for and complete. At the rate that he was going, he wasn't going to ever have time to learn coding. Especially because it wasn't an immediate need for Derrick. However, this was really important to Derrick. He wanted to learn how to code, and to do so, he tried to see why he wasn't achieving his goal. As expected, Derrick quickly figured out that if he really wanted to learn this coding language, he would have to go into isolation mode. Effectively Monk Mode. He decided to go into Monk Mode, though he didn't call it that at the time. He took a vacation to Cuba, and spend four weeks there working in his coding. He made sure to have access to the internet so he could still manage his businesses through email. He let the vice president of his club act as interim president and delegated his other obligations. After four weeks, he was content with the new skill that he had learned. Not only was he able to get through the beginner course, but he had also finished the intermediate course. What the program said would take 8-9 weeks, only took him 4 weeks. All due to the utilization of isolation to his schedule.

Once you have time on your side, you only have yourself as a hurdle.

Friends

Friendships are great, we are social creatures, and we enjoy the company of others. We like to share our joys with other people. This is a healthy part of being human. However, every good thing comes in temperance. Most likely, you have a friend that demands a lot of your time. They want to text, they want to go out, to do activities. They want to gossip. This may not all be negative, but the truth is that there many instances where it is people that we consider friends who are holding us back. They aren't doing it intentionally. But:

"You are the company you keep"

This suggest that it does matter to have people around that pushes you. A rule of thumb for having a good balance of friends is the ⅓ rule.
You want:

> *⅓ of your friends to be inspirational to you*
> *⅓ of your friends to be on par with you*
> *⅓ of your friends to be the inspiration to*

You do not want too much of one category of friends. If you have just low ambitions friends, you are likely to not fully achieve your potential. You may not pick up the right habits. If you have too many people on the same level, you aren't going to learn anything. If you have too many higher level friends, you are going to feel overwhelmed and lose perspective.

During monk mode, you will want your alone time. Ignoring your friends is not necessary, but reducing the frequency of contact is needed. You could even explain to your friends what is going on. You may even be able to discover who are your "real friends":

Samantha decided to go into Monk Mode to save money to pay off her $20,000 student loan. She decided to live frugally for 5 months. She turned off her cable, phone, and even electricity! Her only expenses were food, housing, and gas (just to get to work). She told her friends, at the time, what she planned to do. She also said that she might need their help. They all agreed and said they would help her out in any way shape and form. Unfortunately, Samantha later figured out that this wouldn't be the case.

There were moments where Samantha asked some friends if she could store some perishable food in their fridge, and other times where she asked if she could use their drier for laundry, and some of her "friends" simply refused and were dismissive of her. She was taken aback. It wasn't all of her friends, they were some who truly supported her and gave her the help that she needed. The help was trivial and ranged from things like doing laundry, and occasional food storage. She was very grateful to them. After about 5 months, she was able to save up enough money to pay off her student loan, and she has kept some of the frugalists lifestyle that she took up during Monk Mode. (She went back to using electricity, however)

The point is that friendships can be all-draining and not enough empowering. As you go through Monk Mode, that is something to keep in mind.

Social Media

Social media has been the phenomenon of the last decade. It has been become a buzzword that incite many different emotions. On one part, social media has been able to facilitate tremendous good to society and the global community. People are able to connect now like never before. A person living in California can connect with a person in Japan with no trouble. You don't have to worry about losing touch with someone totally because you can add them on your Facebook page. They will always be but a click away. In the beginning, the social media communication were primarily for one to one exchanges, IM, emailing, etc.. However, once sites that emerged as social networking sites came about, it revolutionized the internet. These social networking sites provided a structure where folks now had the ability to connect with numerous people they know but also be in peripheral contact with the friends of their friends. The quest to build the "friend list" helped push the acceleration of the trend. As the popularity for these sites grew, social media became part of the every common day life. With this, digital life emerged.

Sadly, this digital life has with it as many disadvantages as advantages. One of the disadvantages is privacy. Privacy is impossible in the digital life. Whatever that you are doing online, there is an audience that is watching it. That doesn't mean that the audience cares about your online interactions, but there is no validity to believe that privacy is a reality online. There is no such thing, and it can be dangerous to pretend otherwise. Having a picture of you and your buddies playing beer pong may seem humorous, but maybe not so much for your future employer that is doing a preliminary background check.

Another drawback of social media is that we tend to lose perspective when becoming immersed in it. It becomes difficult to take care of our physical real-world connections; we are so worried about the digital connections. We may even start to take our real-world connection for granted, and put our digital ones on a pedestal.

Social media is neither good or bad, it is about what you do with it. Unfortunately, a lot of people are misusing social media by over-indulgence. It is literally killing their productivity. It becomes a huge distraction. When I worked my summer at retail, I could see this. My fellow employees were too busy looking at what their friends posted on their wall than the job at hand. The work tasks came in second, and social media came in first. Apparently, this wasn't just applicable to my work place. There has been a new industry created to make software blocking social media in the workplace, and it is estimated that the cost of social media distractions loses companies 2.4 billion dollars a year. It is that detrimental to productivity. With this in mind, it is very possible that one of the main causes of someone's lack of productivity comes from their social media obsession.

When in Monk Mode, you will want to radically change your social habits if they are unhealthy. For some people, that may mean blocking their social accounts for the duration of their modes. For others, they may get away with a more temperate approach. I can easily get distracted by Facebook. I don't have many friends on the site, but the ones that I have stay fairly active. They will post story after story. The stories are interesting and eye grabbing. I catch myself clicking on stories and getting lost in them. I have wasted hours on these Facebook posts. It was so detrimental to my productivity that I seriously considered deleting my account. The reason I didn't was because Facebook facilitated my long distance connections and friendships. So instead of deleting the account, I decided to significantly limit my interactions with FB. During Monk Mode, I told myself that I would check Facebook for just 10 minutes a week. I even gave myself the day. Wednesday. That would be the day that I would log in, check in and logout. It became so effective for me that even after Monk Mode, it has become my default practice. I, however, kept the Facebook Messenger App because I use that strictly for communication purposes. You have the freedom to choose the intensity that you are the most comfortable with, but if you spend more than 30 minutes on social media a day, then it has room to be decreased in your life.

Family

Monk Mode may also be a time where you take a break from your family. Family is great and they can be extremely supportive at times. If you have a family like that, then surely keep them around even throughout your Monk Mode. Make sure that they know that you are going into temperate isolation, and may have limited contact with them. If you have family that is inconsiderate, demeaning, and draining, then you will definitely have to take a mental break from them.

The difference between Monk Mode and other isolation modes is that there is never any obligation to ignore or totally eliminate a factor of your life. It is all about reducing everything to a manageable amount. We acknowledge that people have needs and monk mode shouldn't be torture. It shouldn't feel like you are becoming less, you should feel more free and have the ability to do what you think is best for you. You want to see that 24 hours is actually a lot of time to get so things done in the day. You want every activity to be positive and self-developing. There will be things that wants to crunch your time that is not positive or self-developing, and you want to cut those out. Family can sometimes fall into this camp. Family members are people too. They have flaws, and their ideals may not coincide with yours. I believe that you should love your family, no matter what, but this doesn't mean to subjugate yourself to perpetual ridicule.

My cousin, Elaine, had to learn this the hard way. Elaine's direct family has a natural knack for technical knowledge and skills. Elaine's father is a computer engineer. Her mother is a chemistry professor, and her sister's a data analyst. When she was young, Elaine struggled with mathematics and the sciences, but her family encouraged her to study and pursue it. She worked very hard and eventually started to see vast improvement in her scores. By the time that she was in high school, she was scoring in the 80th percentile in her standardized test. It wasn't as good as her sister, but her parents were content. She would be able to get into any middle tier or selective top tier university, and pursue a degree in the STEM field. Elaine had a different idea in mind. While she was happy that her parents were proud of her work ethic in mathematics, her true passion was in music. Her dream was to tour the world and perform in shows. She had no intention of going to college.

When senior year came around, her parents asked her why she hadn't filled out any early college application forms yet. This is when Elaine hit them with the news of her plans. Her parents were not pleased at all. They scolded her, and urged her to give up on the pipe dream immediately. Elaine's mom, who is usually very supportive of Elaine, also did not take her side. She pleaded with Elaine to at least apply to some colleges, as a backup plan. Elaine responded by saying that applying to college would take time and effort away from her primary goal, which was music. The drift in the family grew, to the point where Elaine's father stopped talking to her. During Elaine's high school graduation, none of her direct family were there.

As the years went by, Elaine started to have a small music career. She joined a band, that would travel and perform in gigs. The shows were not big time, or made big bucks, but she was happy to be doing what she loves. Every gig that she could, she invited her family over, and they never came. When she would go visit, her parents would only talk about how she had wasted her potential, and that at the rate that she's going, she will end up homeless and broke. Frustrated with her parent's constant belittling of her, Elaine broke contact from them. It was painful for her, but she felt that it was necessary for her to keep positive vibes around. After six months of her grinding in the music scene, she caught a break, when a cruise vacation agency hired the band to perform full time in their program.

Elaine may have been a bit stubborn, but nonetheless, she decided to go after her dream 100%, and she didn't want any distractions clouding her judgment. She went into monk mode, and grinded her way to a job where she can play music and earn an income at the same time. The perfect scenario for her.

Sometimes, it is necessary to take a mental break from the negativity coming from the people we love. We can never push them out completely, but we can tell ourselves that for a given period of time, we do not want to be around such energy.

Chapter 4

Improvement

Hitherto, the most important part of Monk Mode is the introspection period. The time where you reflect on what you want to change about yourself, or the time where you declare a particular goal. During that process, you wrote down a plan of how you would achieve that goal. There was a timeline, and a list of activities that corresponded to your goal. Now, it's time to put that into action.

The improvement period happens simultaneously with the isolation period. This is when you are actually improving yourself or accomplishing a task. During Monk Mode, you want every hour of your time to be contemplated. Of course, there is always the instances of an emergency, but for the most part, you should be able to follow a strict schedule. As an example, I will show my schedule for when I was in Monk Mode, what you will notice is that every single hour, from the time that I eat, to the time that I head to bed was planned out. I wrote down the times where I would hang out with my family and friends, and the times that where I would be focused on a particular task.

This schedule is from when I went into Monk Mode to prepare for my GRE exams. The GRE, for those who don't know, is the standardized test used to evaluate one's competency to enter and do well in graduate school. The GRE is extremely important because the scores serves as cutoff point for a lot of graduate program. Meaning that the score that you get will indicate the kind of school that will even consider you. It is a beefed up version of the SAT and ACT.
I had to study for this exam, while taking 21 credits.

Schedule

Times	Monday	Tuesday	Wednesday	Thursday	Friday	Saturday	Sunday
5:00 AM	Morning Routine							
6:00 AM	Gre	Homework	Gre	Homework	Gre		
7:00 AM	Breakfast	Breakfast	Breakfast	Breakfast	Breakfast		Gre
8:00 AM	Gre	Homework	Gre	Homework	GRE		Gre
9:00 AM	Gre	Homework	Gre	Gre	Gre	Homework	Gre
10:00 AM	Nap	Meeting	Nap	Gre	Nap	Homework	Gre
11:00 AM	Class I	Lunch	Class I	Nap	Class I	Homework	Gre
12:00 PM	lunch	Hang out with Friends	Lunch	Lunch	Lunch	Lunch	Pick up Basketball
1:00 PM	Class II	Class IV	CLass III	Class IV	Class II	Homework	Pick up Basketball
2:00 PM	Homework	Class V	Homework	Class V	Lab	Homework	Lunch
3:00 PM	Class III	Class VI	Class III	Class VI	Class III	GRE	Homework
4:00 PM	Homework	Gre		Relax	Hangout	GRE	Homework
5:00 PM	Homework	Gre	b/m	Dinner	Hangout	GRE	Homework
6:00 PM	Dinner	Pick up Basketball	Pick up Basketball		Hangout	GRE	Work Study
7:00 PM	Dinner	Pick up Basketball	Pick up basketball		Hangout	Dinner	Work Study
8:00 PM	Pick up basketball	Homework	Workout	Pick up basketball	Hangout	Gre	Work Stuy
9:00 PM	Pick up basketball	Homework	Dinner	Hangout	Hangout	Relax	Work Study
10:00 PM	Workout	Homework	Relax	Relax	Hangout	Relax	
11:00 PM	Relax	Relax	Relax	relax		Relax	
12:00 AM	Evening Routine	Evening Routine	Evening routine	evening routine			
1:00 AM							
2:00 AM							
3:00 AM							

As mentioned and seen on the last page, my schedule was for the most part fixed. If I had an emergency, I would take care of that and adjust my schedule. This schedule was very hard in the beginning but it's a schedule that I followed for two whole months. It provided great results, as I got high enough scores to satisfy top tier universities. I also tried to not totally sacrifice my social life, because those ties helped me in motivation and brought me balance. I made sure to only hang out people that were positive, and not draining. This schedule can be altered to achieve any goal. If you want to lose weight, make a plan and fill out your day with your obligations. Make sure that you stay realistic. Since I was in college, I didn't have to input meal preparation time (all the meals were made for me), I didn't have to clean my room or bathroom (the school took care of that too), so in short, I had most of my basic needs taken care of for me. Instead of classes, many people will have to work, and they will have to schedule other obligations in there. That is fine, every schedule will be different. Just do not let any junk activity infiltrate your schedule.

Persevere

Do not give up. You know the reason why you went into Monk Mode. You have a goal in mind, you wanted to achieve something. Maybe you are kickstarting a business, and you need to sacrifice your social life for a while during the starting stages. Whatever your goals are, remind yourself of what you are doing and why. Make sure that you get a constant stream of motivation going through you during the day. Have an inspirational quote pop from your laptop every morning, have a screensaver that puts a smile of determination in your face. Keep friends around that are successful and can provide tips and motivation for you. You will feel low at some point, but the difference between those who are successful and those who aren't are that the successful ones went past their limits to combat the low times. You have that potential too, if you are able to contemplate going through something as rigorous as Monk Mode, then you have the potential to be great. To be successful in your niche. All you have to do is persevere!

Chapter 5
Leaving Monk Mode

When do you leave monk mode?

When you are satisfied with your overall progress. There are lessons that will be learned as you go through Monk Mode. These lessons are going to stay and propel you to success. One of the biggest lessons that you will learn by going through this process is self-discipline. You will become a master in knowing how to keep yourself in check, and staying accountable. This discipline will be available to you during other endeavors and facets of your life. If you decided that you want to save up money to buy a car, you know that you have a process where you can make a plan, stick to it, and you will see results. If you are looking for a job, you know that perseverance and an open mind will dramatically increase your probability of finding a quality occupation.

Another lesson you will learn is that time is extremely precious. I remember my days in high school, where I could watch hours and hours of television without a care in the world. Many working class adults do this even to this day. And though occasional television can be relaxing and even beneficial, the average American watches 33 hours of televisions. That is more than a FULL day of just sitting and watching mind numbing media. When you go into Monk Mode, you will learn that these hours can be used to do greater things. During those hours you could have learned how to prepare meals, instrument playing, language, or have spent time with your significant other. Every hour count, and once in Monk Mode, you will realize this.

When you come out of Monk Mode, you will have your friends asking you to participate in time wasting activities. Having a heightened sensitivity to time, you will be able to recognize activities that are worthwhile, and those that are not. If your friends want to have a binge ice cream and Netflix night, you will be able to see the detrimental aspects of that activity. You may even be able to suggest an alternate activity that is fun and provides overall benefits, like running a marathon.

The one mistake that is made when one leaves Monk Mode is that it is easy to become complacent. You may have made significant progress during Monk Mode, and have become far ahead of your peers. You may feel good about yourself and decide to relax. That would be a major mistake, you can never become complacent. You always have to be in search of bettering yourself and the people around you. The hunger must still be there to achieve the next goal. This book applies to everyone, but only the truly ambitious people will take MM to the next level. They have ambitious that requires extreme focus and an abnormal sense of direction. Do not relapse back into mediocrity. Keep improving yourself.

I do not think that Monk Mode is a state that should be kept permanently. It is a very rigorous attempt to achieving a goal. It is that grind time that a lot of successful people have gone through to break the plateau. Monk Mode is a powerful tool, but being in that state for too long can affect your life in irreparable ways. If you like the feeling of being in Monk Mode, and would like to have a lifestyle that is similar (though not as intense as MM) I would suggest to look into minimalism. I am a minimalist myself, and I get all of the benefits of both being in Monk Mode and still having access to the world. Meaning that I don't adhere to the strict isolation rules that Monk Mode requires, but I have also taken habits from MM and incorporated into my life. Minimalism has allowed me to reach an even higher balance than just being in Monk Mode. Monk Mode is a tool that I still use when I feel overwhelmed and need to get a particular project done, but overall, minimalism can bring simplicity and happiness to your life. To know more about the minimalist philosophy, I give a brief overview below:

Minimalism is the philosophy that by owning less stuff, you will be happier. It is a philosophy that gives a reverse relationship between the amount of things you own, and the amount of freedom that you feel. The less objects you own, the more you will be. It is in direct contrast with the philosophy dominating the western world, materialism. Materialism teaches that the more you consume and aggregate, the better your life will be. It is a philosophy that has permeated and is on display every day. Just walk to your local supermarket. Minimalism is in direct opposition towards that. It is about removing the clutter from your life, so that you can see clearly. And minimalism isn't just restricted to objects, it can be applied to spirituality, relationships, and diet.

I will be releasing a book on Minimalism in the coming months. Please stay tuned for further releases.

In conclusion, thank you for reading through this book Monk Mode, I hope that you have found it encouraging and worthwhile.

Printed in Great Britain
by Amazon